VICTORIAN BRITAIN

BY

JOHN GUY

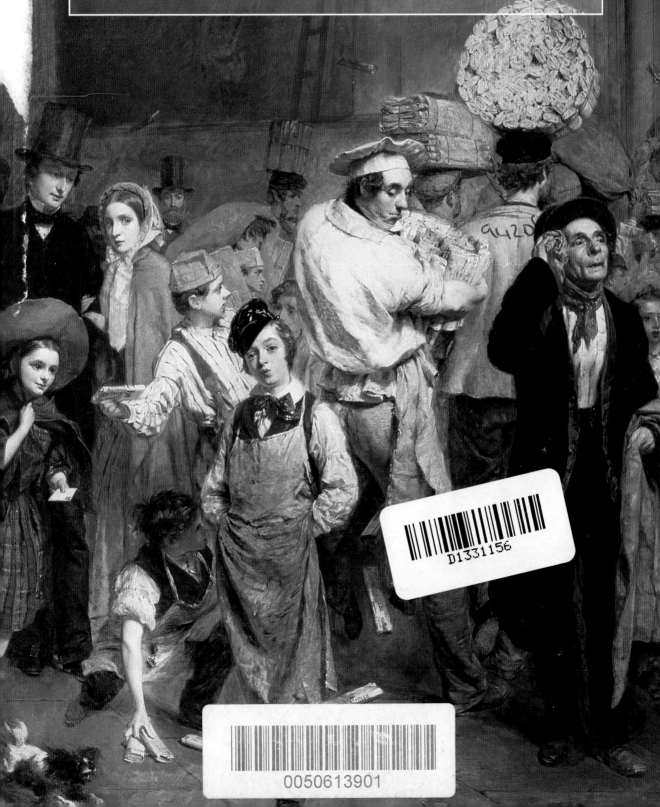

COUNTRY LIFE

While new technology and machinery improved how many farms worked, for most people the industrial revolution of the 18th and 19th centuries was a period of great social change. Many people lost their jobs and their homes at the same time, because most houses were tied to their jobs. This meant they were forced to seek work elsewhere.

NEW MACHINERY

New machinery, such as this steam traction engine, was very useful and could do the work of several men. In just a few years heavy horses, that had been used to pull ploughs and other farm machinery, were no longer needed.

ANIMAL HUSBANDRY

While those involved in farming suffered enormously at the hands of 'progress', cattle herders and shepherds were not affected by the technological changes sweeping the land – their roles could not be done by machines.

COUNTRY AIR

Although many of those who worked in the country still lived in very basic, one-roomed cottages, living conditions and sanitation were much better than in town slums.

CHANGING MARKETPLACE

Many villages lost their weekly market as more and more of the food produced was taken to the towns to feed their growing populations. A single village shop, selling a range of goods, could usually supply most rural communities.

LIFE EXPECTANCY

Although generally poorer than town dwellers, those who lived in the country usually had a better quality of life and could expect to live longer – about 50 years of age compared to 40 for those in towns.

OUR DAILY BREAD

In 1815 Corn Laws had been passed to keep grain prices high and protect England from cheap imports, but these were repealed in 1846 to allow free trade. The result was a fall in the price of bread, though farmers were affected badly as a result.

LIFE IN TOWNS

At the beginning of Victoria's reign (1837) only about 20 percent of the population lived in towns. By 1901, when she died, this figure had risen to about 75 percent. During this same period the population of Britain doubled from around 20 million to 40 million. Most people moved to towns to find work in the factories. Rows of poor-quality terraced slums were built around the factories to house workers.

VICTIMS OF CIRCUMSTANCE

Poverty turned many people to crime in the dingy towns. The old and infirm often fell victim to pickpockets as this cartoon shows.

POOR SANITATION

Sanitary conditions in Victorian towns were often very bad. Only the rich could afford proper toilet facilities. The poor had to share a lavatory – usually just a shed over a hole in the ground treated with quicklime to dissolve waste. Few houses had running water or drains.

HOMELESSNESS

Homelessness was a constant problem in towns, especially for those who were unable to work, and were literally put out on to the streets. Alcohol was cheap (beer was less than 1p per pint) and easier to find than good drinking water, so drunkenness was a problem, even amongst children.

STREET TRADERS

Traders sold their wares, such as bread, milk and pies, from handcarts on the streets. Girls might sell cut flowers while boys might offer a shoe shine.

COMPARATIVE LIFESTYLES

These two views show the difference between the poor and wealthy sectors of 19th-century towns. The rich could afford elegant, well-built homes, while the poor had to live in cramped, back-to-back housing surrounded by noise and filth.

THE HIGH LIFE

Wealthy young ladies went to balls, parties, the opera and the theatre, in order to meet young men they might marry.

The Victorian age saw the development of a new middle class, wealthy businessmen who made vast fortunes from the new advances in technology. This was often at the expense of the working classes who were forced to work in bad conditions for low wages. Until the industrial revolution, most of the country's wealth was in land ownership, particularly the estates of the aristocracy, but now anyone could become rich.

A STITCH IN TIME

New technology and mass-production brought many labour-saving devices, including the sewing machine. This sewing machine, made by Wheeler and Wilson, revolutionized clothes manufacture.

QUEEN VICTORIA

- *Born 1819*
- *Came to the throne 1837*
- *Died 1901*

Victoria was proud of the technical achievements of her reign, and allowed many inventions to be used in the royal household, such as electric lighting and carpet cleaners.

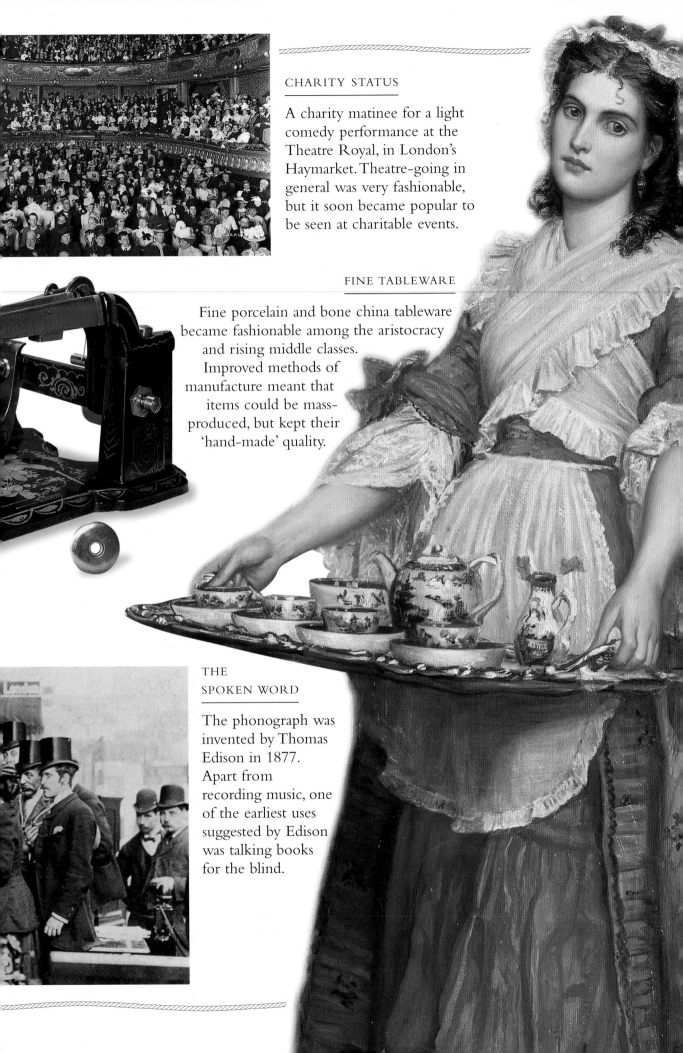

CHARITY STATUS

A charity matinee for a light comedy performance at the Theatre Royal, in London's Haymarket. Theatre-going in general was very fashionable, but it soon became popular to be seen at charitable events.

FINE TABLEWARE

Fine porcelain and bone china tableware became fashionable among the aristocracy and rising middle classes. Improved methods of manufacture meant that items could be mass-produced, but kept their 'hand-made' quality.

THE SPOKEN WORD

The phonograph was invented by Thomas Edison in 1877. Apart from recording music, one of the earliest uses suggested by Edison was talking books for the blind.

THE POOR AT HOME

Although the technological revolution brought wealth to some, it brought poverty to the working classes. Many were forced to work long hours, in dreadful conditions, for low wages. Many chose to emigrate to Australia, America and Canada. One way out of the 'poverty trap' was to work in service in the houses of the wealthy. There were over one million domestic servants in 1851 out of a population of just 20 million.

POVERTY

Many of the homeless lived in workhouses where, in payment for working during the day, they received a meal and a bed. This old woman could not work, and slept on the steps of the workhouse. She looked after a friend's baby in return for food.

CHILDREN'S HOMES

Homelessness was an ever-growing problem in towns, particularly among children whose parents might have died. Dr Thomas Barnado opened his first home for poor boys in London in 1870. Many of them had run away to escape the cruelty of factory conditions. Dr Barnado gave them food and shelter.

PAWNBROKERS

In an age before pensions and welfare benefits, if a poor family fell upon hard times they were forced to sell or 'pawn' their possessions. This was especially true for widows whose incomes stopped when their husband died.

LEARNING BY HEART

Few working-class children were educated in case it made them unhappy with their life. Some however went to dame schools – run by women in their own homes, where reading, writing and simple arithmetic were taught.

COTTAGE INDUSTRIES

It was not unusual for poor couples to have as many as 9 or 10 children. Although this view shows a typical family with the children at play – probably on a Sunday, the only day of rest – the whole family was expected to work. Even children not sent out to work, had to help by doing jobs around the house or making items for sale.

FOOD AND DRINK

One of the biggest problems facing Victorian society was how to feed a growing population. In pre-industrial Britain, the majority of people worked on the land and produced their own food. Most people now worked in factories and had to buy all their food with what little wages they received.

DELIVERED TO YOUR DOOR

Milk was delivered straight from the farm. Customers took their jugs out into the street to the milkman, who filled them from large churns.

GREATER CHOICE

Never before had such a range of foods been available, as cheap imports came in from abroad. Even the basic diets of the poor gradually improved and became more varied. Tea, once a luxury drink, could now be afforded by most people.

COLD FOODS

One of the solutions to keeping food fresh was this dry-air syphon refrigerator (c.1900). Food was chilled by ice blocks in a compartment next to it. Towards the end of the Victorian era tinned foods also became available.

HOME DELIVERIES

In smaller towns, and villages, street tradesmen still carried their goods from door to door. Fresh bread, fish, dairy produce and vegetables were often sold this way. However, in larger towns, improved standards of hygiene meant that more and more people bought their food from shops.

THE MIDDLE MAN

Markets have survived from the pre-industrialized age, when there were few shops, and buyers and sellers met to exchange goods. At town wholesale markets, such as Covent Garden fruit and vegetable market in London (shown here), larger traders bought goods in bulk, and then sold them on to smaller traders for a profit.

PASTIMES

For most people, Sunday was the only day when they did not have to work, so many simply rested. For others, cheap railway transport meant that for the first time they could visit other areas. Day trips to seaside towns became popular, as did visits to the growing number of public art galleries and museums.

A GAME FOR GENTLEMEN

Cricket, first played in the 16th century, grew in popularity and became a gentleman's pursuit. W.G. Grace, (perhaps the most famous cricketer of all time) lifted the game to its present status. He had a playing career of 35 years and on one occasion gained the score of 224 not out.

CHILDREN'S ENTERTAINMENT

Children in the country were sometimes treated to a performance by a travelling puppeteer with his 'Punch and Judy' show.

THE NEWLY RICH

Industrialization had created a new class of businessmen with lots of money to spend. Gambling had always been popular but now new casinos and gentlemen's clubs made it respectable.

I SAY, I SAY, I SAY...

Every town had at least one, and sometimes more, theatres and music halls, showing everything from variety shows to plays, opera and ballet. In the 1890s over 350 music halls opened in London alone.

FOR ALL CLASSES

Gambling on sporting events had always been popular, and the Victorians loved it. It was one of the rare occasions when people from different backgrounds mixed socially.

TRADITIONAL SKILLS

Traditional needlework and embroidery skills remained the main pastime for many middle- and upper-class ladies. This design is from the title page of a children's book on dolls' houses, which became extremely popular in Victorian times.

BESIDE THE SEASIDE

The benefits of sea bathing had been discovered in the 18th century, but it was the railway age that made seaside trips possible for the masses.

FASHION

By about 1870,
bustles replaced
crinoline. Skirts
were draped over
a frame of padded
cushions to give
more fullness to
the back of
the dress.

The rich liked to dress in the latest fashions. They could afford good-quality materials and enjoyed wearing clothes to look good, even though they were often very uncomfortable. The poor wore more practical clothes, suitable for their work and living conditions, and not taking fashion into account very much. People from all classes usually kept a special set of clothes for their 'Sunday best'.

FASHION CONSCIOUSNESS

Narrow waists were very fashionable for ladies, right up to the end of Queen Victoria's reign. This was achieved by wearing corsets made of steel, wood or bone. These were laced so tightly that they made breathing difficult, causing some women to faint.

FASHION ACCESSORIES

Ladies carried many fashion accessories, particularly when attending social functions. As well as jewellery, they might carry a decorated fan, such as the one shown here. Hairstyles were complicated, often including wigs and false hair pieces. Gentlemen usually carried gloves and a walking cane.

FOLLOWERS OF FASHION

Working-class children wore cast-offs or cut-down adult clothes. Wealthier families dressed their children very formally in miniature versions of adult styles. Boys and girls both wore dresses until they were about five years old.

CHANGING FACE OF FASHION

The invention of the sewing machine did not make seamstresses, tailors and shoemakers redundant, but instead made more elaborate designs possible. Ladies' shoes in particular became far more daring in their design. Gentlemen wore spats, – short cloth gaiters below their trouser bottoms – to protect their shoes from mud.

COSTUME JEWELLERY

Many precious and semi-precious stones were imported from India, and used to decorate items of fashion jewellery.

ART AND ARCHITECTURE

Charles Dickens (1812-70) was the greatest and most popular novelist of his day. His clear descriptions of Victorian Britain give us a good idea of what life was really like, particularly for the poor. All of his books were serialized, making them available to all classes.

*V*ictorian art and architecture was often unfairly criticized for producing nothing new and original. The Victorians produced Gothic and Classical revivals, but they also built graceful structures, such as bridges and canopies, using iron, steel and glass in their own style. Writers such as Charles Dickens, Sir Walter Scott and the Brontë sisters developed the art of novel writing, and the most original group of English painters, the Pre-Raphaelites formed a school of art that reflected Victorian thinking.

THE CRYSTAL PALACE

The Great Exhibition of 1851 was Prince Albert's idea and was housed in the purpose-built Crystal Palace. It was a masterpiece of cast iron and glass designed by Joseph Paxton. It was three times the length of St Paul's Cathedral. The building survived a move from Hyde Park to Sydenham after the exhibition, but sadly burned down in 1936.

Many art galleries
and museums
opened in towns
throughout Britain.
They introduced
ordinary people
to the wider
world of art.

TRAGIC GENIUS

The Brontë sisters – Anne, Emily and Charlotte –
all wrote under male pseudonyms to improve
their chances of success. They lived a lonely
life on the Yorkshire moors and all died at
young ages.

HEALTH AND MEDICINE

*T*he main cause of health problems facing Victorians, particularly in the towns, was that of overcrowding. The large numbers of people living in the crowded slum houses created a lot of waste, but there was no proper way to get rid of it. Streets became open sewers, which led to many outbreaks of diseases such as typhoid and cholera. A series of Public Health Acts from 1848 made it the responsibility of local councils to provide drainage and clean water supplies and clear slums.

THE WATER CLOSET

As sewage systems improved, rich households put in flushable toilets. The poor usually shared an 'earth closet' outside, which was often moved as it filled up.

MEDIEVAL CURES

Before around 1856 when scientists such as Louis Pasteur found that disease was caused by microscopic bacteria, medicine had made little progress since the Middle Ages. Basic treatments, such as blood-letting to remove poisons and infections, were still widely practised.

SHOCK TACTICS

In 1867 Joseph Lister developed an antiseptic to kill bacteria, which greatly increased the survival rate from surgery. Before that, over half of patients died from shock, gangrene or other infections.

POOR DIET

Many children, who did not get enough sunlight, fresh air and healthy food, developed a disease called rickets. This caused their bones – especially in their legs – to bend. Vitamin D, from milk, helped prevent it.

WATERBORNE DISEASES

Following many outbreaks of typhoid and cholera in overcrowded towns, Edwin Chadwick discovered a link between disease and poor living conditions. Huge sewers were built to improve drainage and to carry dirty water out to sea.

DENTAL HYGIENE

This Victorian dentist's surgery shows treadle-operated drills. The successful use of chloroform as an anaesthetic after 1847 made it possible to remove teeth or perform other operations painlessly.

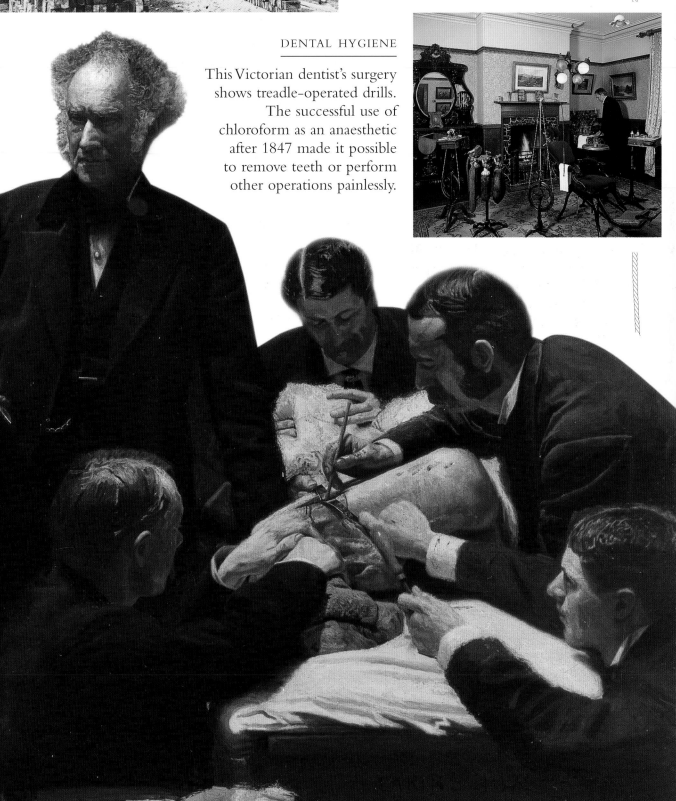

LOVE AND MARRIAGE

ARRANGED MARRIAGES

Few marriages were love matches, but were arranged by parents who chose a suitable partner for their children.

Women from all classes were expected to marry young (usually about age 18) and to raise a family, and they were not expected to have a career. Upper- and middle-class girls were not usually allowed to meet with young men on their own. If a woman had a child when single she was scorned by society and might be disowned by her family, forced to enter a workhouse in order to survive.

TO DISTANT SHORES

Many professionals and members of the armed forces were sent out to various parts of the empire. Wives were left to bring up their families alone. Here a wife says goodbye to her husband before he sets sail.

FUN BEFORE MARRIAGE

Young, single men from wealthy families were often encouraged to have fun with lower-class girls. However, marriage between people from different classes was frowned upon and could lead to the wealthy partner being cut off from his or her family.

A SPINSTER'S LIFE

Unmarried women were regarded as the property of their fathers, who could also claim any wages they earned. Most parents, however, wanted to see their children married off, particularly daughters, who might have no income should anything happen to their fathers.

ROYAL PROPOSAL

According to the rules followed by royalty, no man is allowed to propose to a queen, so Victoria had to ask for Albert's hand in marriage. She is seen here surrounded by her children and grandchildren.

WOMEN AND CHILDREN

LIFE OF EASE

While boys from wealthy families were trained for a profession, girls were not expected to work. They spent their time entertaining, or making social calls to friends and neighbours.

Life for women and children in the 19th century could be very hard, and the poor had little chance of improving matters. Social reformers, such as Lord Shaftesbury, worked to make things better, and a series of Acts was passed in the 1840s reducing the working day to 10 hours and improving conditions. However, some greedy employers ignored the new laws.

COMPULSORY EDUCATION

In 1870 the government passed an Education Act stating that all children between the ages of 5 and 10 must attend school. The education was not free though, and many poorer families could not afford to send their children. After 1891 schooling became free to all.

VALUABLE 'PROPERTIES'

Women of all classes were
regarded as the property
of their husbands, as were
any wages they earned.
Until the Property Act of 1882
all of a woman's property automatically
belonged to her husband.

IMPRISONED BY CIRCUMSTANCE

Many women were
forced to take their
children to prison
with them if
convicted of a crime,
rather than abandon
them. Prison
reformer, Elizabeth
Fry helped to improve
the dreadful
conditions inside, and
helped set up schools
for the children.

CHILD WORKERS

Childhood in Victorian times was short.
Children were considered the property of
their father, who could send them out to
work as young as five years old, and keep
all their wages to help support the family.

WOMEN'S RIGHTS?

Women had few
rights in 19th-
century Britain, and
had to perform the
same tasks as men at
work, but for much
less pay. This picture was
taken at an iron foundry in
South Wales in 1865.

WAR AND WEAPONRY

After their victory over Napoleon at Waterloo, the British army were unprepared for the harsh conditions of the Crimean War with Russia (1854-56). Following this, Britain concentrated on either extending or defending the empire, which covered one-quarter of the world's land mass – the largest empire ever known.

NEW TECHNOLOGY

Methods of warfare changed greatly during the 19th century. New technology developed better weapons, such as this rapid-firing gatling gun of 1870.

EMPIRE BUILDING

With rising poverty and unemployment at home, there was no shortage of volunteers to sign up for the military. Men chose to risk their lives and perhaps die abroad rather than dying penniless at home.

THE INDIAN MUTINY

Since the 18th century the East India Company had run India, with help from the army and Indian troops. In 1857 the native troops, supported by many Indian princes, rebelled against British rule. The rebellion was crushed, and afterwards India was placed under the direct rule of the British government.

GUERRILLA WARFARE

In 1899 war broke out in South Africa between Dutch settlers – the Boers – and the British. A massive army was sent to crush them, but it proved ineffective against the Boers' guerrilla tactics. Peace was only eventually achieved in 1902.

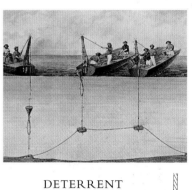

DETERRENT

Alfred Nobel, a Swedish scientist, invented dynamite and other explosives, for use in civil engineering projects and as a deterrent to help achieve world peace. However, military powers, including Britain, used them to make weapons, such as sea mines used to blow up ships.

VALLEY OF DEATH

The 'Charge of the Light Brigade' at Balaclava in the Crimea in 1854, was one of Britain's worst military disasters. Confused orders and bad officers ended in a charge straight towards the Russian guns. Nearly half of the 673 cavalrymen died or were wounded.

CRIME AND PUNISHMENT

With so much poverty and dreadful living conditions, many people turned to crime. Punishments were severe, even for children. You could be imprisoned for stealing a loaf of bread. Prisons became full, so 'hulks' were moored in river estuaries to house prisoners. Many convicts were also sent to the colonies.

MORAL STANDARDS

Victorians were very moral. This music hall dancer was imprisoned for three months for wearing this costume in public.

ROYAL SCAPEGOAT

Many people blamed Queen Victoria for their hardships and several attempts were made on her life. This attempt was by an out-of-work Irishman in 1849.

DEATH PENALTY

At the beginning of the 19th century over 200 crimes were punishable by death. Despite reforms, there were still over 70 crimes carrying the death sentence in Victorian times, including petty theft and assault.

WHEEL OF MISFORTUNE

Conditions inside Victorian prisons were crowded and very basic. Treadmills, like the one shown here, were used to punish unruly prisoners.

A POLICEMAN'S LOT

Until the reform bills of Sir Robert Peel in the 1820s, when a proper police force was set up in London, many criminals got away unpunished. By early Victorian times most towns had their own police force, often ex-soldiers and run like the army.

TRANSPORT AND SCIENCE

Britain's scientists and engineers led the world with their inventions, such as the development of steam and internal combustion engines, electricity and building techniques. Many familiar household objects today, such as light bulbs, typewriters, packaged food and hi-fi had their origins in the Victorian age. Britain became known as the 'workshop of the world'.

SMILE!

Cameras, first developed in the 19th century, were for the first time in history able to record events as they happened. At first they were used for reconnaissance (exploration) by the army.

IMPROVED ROADS

The first motorcars (invented c.1865) looked like horseless carriages and were open-topped. They needed surface roads to run on. This led to road improvements, including the development of tarmacadam (tarmac) for roadsurfacing.

UNDERWATER TACTICS

The development of the submarine and self-propelled torpedoes in both Britain and France changed fighting techniques. The one shown here, invented by the Rev. G.W. Garret in 1880, was launched on rails.

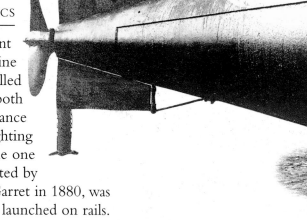

ON THE RIGHT TRACK

The Victorian age saw the rapid development of railways. For the first time in history fast, cheap transport was available to everyone, making travel much easier. Between 1829 and 1900 around 35,400 kilometres of track were laid in Britain, and in 1863 the world's first underground railway was opened in London.

MASS-PRODUCTION

Advances in technology meant that it was possible to mass-produce many items for everyday use. Before, they had been hand-made, which s expensive, like this practical tape measure.

IT'S GOOD TO TALK

The telephone was invented by Alexander Graham Bell in 1875. This exciting development was very expensive, only the rich could afford it. You could not dial direct and had to go through an operator. Businessmen, were quick to see how useful the telephone could be and how it improved communications.

RELIGION

Until Victorian times, most Christians believed that God created the world exactly as it said in the Bible. So, when Charles Darwin and others challenged this view with their new theories of evolution, they shattered the beliefs of ordinary people and some of the clergy. Many people struggled with their religious beliefs and the new scientific theories. Darwin was scorned for his theories all his life.

CHALLENGE TO THE CHURCH

The biologist Charles Huxley supported Darwin's theories of evolution when the Church attacked his views and tried to discredit him.

SUNDAY SCHOOLS

For many working-class children – who worked all week – Sunday or charity schools, organized by the Church, were the only form of education they received. Apart from learning to read, the only other subject usually taught was Bible studies.

The Victorians were highly religious and very moral. For the first time since the Reformation many new churches were built, or medieval ones restored. At the beginning of Victoria's reign (1837) about 60 percent of the population regularly went to church on Sundays; today the figure is less than one percent.

THE DESCENT OF MAN

When Charles Darwin published *The Origin of Species* in 1859, he was challenging the account of creation from the Bible in which God created man in his own likeness. According to Darwin, man evolved gradually from an ape-like creature over many millions of years.

THE 'SALLY ARMY'

The self-styled 'General' William Booth founded the Salvation Army in 1878. Originally a Methodist preacher, he modelled his church along army lines to combat drunkenness, and exploitation of women and the working classes. He also helped ex-prisoners and introduced legal aid for the poor.

THE OXFORD MOVEMENT

Evangelicalism started in Oxford. A group of Anglicans felt that the Church was not carrying out its duties to the poor. They formed a new church with a more caring approach.

GLOSSARY

Blood-letting It was wrongly believed that by withdrawing blood, some diseases could be cured or prevented.

Bustle A pad or frame worn beneath the skirt which puffs it out at the back.

Census An official survey of the public.

Chloroform A type of anaesthetic popular in Victorian times.

Cholera A serious infectious disease which effects the intestines. It is caused by eating or drinking something infected with the bacteria.

Disowned Refusing to acknowledge or be associated with someone.

Gangrene A serious infection caused by bacteria in a wound. It causes the skin to rot and can lead to death.

Pawn Leaving an object with a pawnbroker in return for them lending you money.

Pseudonym A false name sometimes used by authors.

Typhoid A serious infectious disease which causes a fever, red spots over the chest, and severe pain. It is caused by bacteria and was often deadly at this time.

ACKNOWLEDGEMENTS

We would like to thank: Graham Rich, Tracey Pennington, Liz Rowe, Rosie Hankin and Peter Done for their assistance.
Copyright © 2008 *ticktock* Entertainment Ltd.
Published by *ticktock* Media Ltd, Unit 2, Orchard Business Centre North Farm Road, Tunbridge Wells, Kent TN2 3XF, U.K.
All rights reserved. No part of this publication may be reproduced, stored in a retrieval system, or transmitted in any form or by any means electronic, mechanical, photocopying, recording or otherwise, without prior written permission of the copyright owner.
A CIP catalogue record for this book is available from the British Library.
ISBN 978 1 84696 658 3
Picture research by Image Select.
Printed in China.

Picture Credits:
t=top, b=bottom, c=centre, l=left, r=right, OFC=outside front cover, IFC=inside front cover, IBC=inside b

The Games Room, 1889, Jean Beraud © ADAGP, Paris and DACS, London 1997 (Musee Carnavalet, Paris/Giraudon/B
By courtesy of BT Archives; 29cr & OBC. B.T. Batsford Ltd; 6/7b. Barnado's Photographic Archive (D58); 8bl & OBC. The Beamish. The N
Library, University of Oxford; John Johnson Collection; Political General folder 1;4l, 5br & 32., Trades and Possessions 6; 4/5b, Educational 16;
Scraps 7; 18l & OBC, Food 2; 18cb, Alphabets 3; 30/31t. Sheffield City Art Galleries/Bridgeman Art Library, London; OFCc. FORBES Maga
London; 6bl & OBC, 21cr, 31tr. Christopher Wood Gallery, London/Bridgeman Art Library, London; 9tl; 12/13b. Marylebone Cricket Club, L
Jefferson College, Philadelphia/Bridgeman Art Library, London; 19b. Getty/English School/Bridgeman Art Library 13cl, Guildhall Art Galle
London; 20b. Mary Evans Picture Library; 3tl, 3tr, 3c, 5tl, 5tr, 12cr, 13cr, 16tl & OBC. By courtesy of Fine Art Photographic Library; 15tr, 16/
Art Photographic Library; 8/9b, 11t. Haynes Fine Art/Fine Art Photographic Library; 6t. Hollywood Road Gallery/Fine Art Photographic Libr
Library; 7r. Polak Gallery/Fine Art Photographic Library; 13t, 22tl, 22bl. Sutcliffe Galleries/Fine Art Photographic Library; 3br, 21tl. Guildhall
John Hillelson Collection; 8tl, 26cr. Hulton Getty; 2l 7tl, 14tl, 19tl, 21br, 27cl, 30tl. Hunting Aerofims Ltd (Mills 147); 13br & OFC. The Illustr
London; IFC/1, 14/15t, 14/15b & OFC, 15br. By courtesy of the National Portrait Gallery, London; 17cr. Oxfordshire Photographic Archive
History Centre, University of Reading; 11cb. The Salvation Army International Heritage Centre; 31br. Science Museum /Science & Society P
28/29b, 29c.

Every effort has been made to trace the copyright holders and we apologize in advance for any u
We would be pleased to insert the appropriate acknowledgement in any subsequent edition